How Did the Wheel Fall Off the Roller Coaster?

How Did the Wheel Fall Off the Roller Coaster?

Confessions of an Inspector

Frank Snowden-Brubaker

Library of Congress Control Number:		2015918852
ISBN:	Hardcover	978-1-5144-2520-6
	Softcover	978-1-5144-2519-0
	eBook	978-1-5144-2518-3

Print information available on the last page.

Rev. date: 11/11/2015

To order additional copies of this book, contact:
Xlibris
1-888-795-4274
www.Xlibris.com
Orders@Xlibris.com
722067

CONTENTS

PRELUDE

AFTER I HAD written this book, but before it had gone to print, a couple of things happened in the news that I couldn't just let go, and I had to somehow include them.

Who could imagine that human beings are capable of doing these things to each other?

Knowingly and purposely poisoning an entire population—from within.

Knowingly and purposely poisoning an entire planet—again from within. With complete disregard to themselves, their fellow man, and the generations to follow, with only one common goal: profit margin!

I'm not talking about religious terrorists. I'm talking about corporate terrorists. Peanut butter executives that knowingly put tainted product on the grocery store shelves. They could have poisoned their own friends and family! Car manufacturers that designed a computer chip to give false readings to pass the emissions test. And these are not the exceptions to the rule! Although these particular actions have extreme consequences, this mind-set is common practice, being conducted on a regular basis by much of upper management. And when I say much, I mean too many of the companies I have personally worked for.

What common man, typical worker, cog in the wheel could even think of doing these types of things to their fellow man? I can't imagine. This is more like a secret-agent-spy thriller, complete with super villains hell-bent on destroying the world, straight out of a Hollywood blockbuster. And given the direction the world is headed, it can't get better; it can only get worse. So it has to be contained. And the only way to contain it is to monitor *them*.

Companies where their best interests are served by catching rejects and failures are choosing profits and short cuts over doing the right thing. Does it sound like I'm a little over the top? It does to me. But these things are in the news right now as I am writing this. They are not made-up, and yes, I am trying to inspire people, to motivate everyone to join me in my cause to remove the decision making from the executives and put it in the hands of the people who just want to do their jobs—engineers, designers, production workers, and, close to my heart, inspectors.

PREFACE

FIRST OF ALL, I would like to state that this is not an indictment against my fellow inspectors. Many are placed in a position where they have to do what the boss says for fear of being fired if they don't. For that matter, the machinists, foremen, and office personnel all have to succumb to similar pressures as the ones placed on the inspectors.

Or maybe it's just me. Maybe I've had a string of bad luck and this book is not representative of the machining world at large but more, just a few bad apples that I've had to deal with in my years as an inspector.

I have had no less than twenty-three jobs since 1978 because I wouldn't conform and be a team player. Thirty-five years of working in machine shops, mostly as an inspector, and some of those years as a machinist.

I would also like to state that I am testifying not about any specific roller-coaster incident, bridge collapsing, etc., but more about the machining world in general and as it relates to me.

Early in my career I was fortunate enough to work with a person who taught a class in geometric tolerancing for his night job, so I was tutored while we worked together. Several years after I worked with him, I began to wonder if I had misunderstood some of the things he taught me. The prints didn't seem to be drawn correctly. So I decided to get formal training, and that was when I realized that many of these blueprints were in error. They were drawn wrong.

Over the years, I have been put into positions where I had to falsify documents, either on inspection reports or on a certificate of conformance. I had to record results that I had no way of verifying because the company just didn't have the proper inspection equipment, or I would record numbers that were not accurate because "the customers won't accept the parts if the numbers are out." I would try to use verbiage when I could so that I wasn't stating actual numbers but stated yes, the findings were within the required tolerance zones, even though they weren't or even if I couldn't and didn't measure them.

If you believe that what I did was wrong, I agree—it was wrong. In my defense, when I was asked to do things that I felt uncomfortable with, that was when I would start looking for another job. But in the meantime, I couldn't just quit and walk out the door. I had bills to pay, just like everybody else. So I would do what I had to until I could get out and find "that honest employer."

When I first started inspecting, it was more "fit, form, and function." Will it assemble? Does it look good, and will it work? What else mattered, right? So what if some dimensions got a little out of tolerance? If it worked, it worked!

And that's how it starts. It's easy to justify accepting parts that don't meet the blueprints perfectly if you know in your heart they will work. You justify it by saying "The tolerance is way too tight. It'll work just fine."

(I have a running gag: "The new engineering graduates are only given four inches of tolerance for their entire careers, and they don't want to use it up all at once.")

But in today's world, if you are required to give results to each and every dimension, then stating "OK" or "Pass" just doesn't cut it.

And when you are repeatedly finding mistakes on blueprints, it's easy to second-guess the engineer that drew it up. Yes, I have been exposed to an overabundance of poorly drawn blueprints. There was one major company that decided to just make up their own symbols—like there weren't any rules they had to follow.

I just want to give a small example for the techies out there: There are symbols used for a specific type of identifying tolerances on a print called geometric tolerancing. Two diagonal, parallel lines is called parallelism. A circle inside a circle is called concentricity. And a circle with crosshairs through it is called true position. This one is used for calling out the target area for locations of features.

This worldwide-recognized company took the true position symbol and elongated the circle into a rectangle with rounded corners when they were locating a slot's position.

I couldn't imagine how they thought that they could just change the symbol! Plus the fact that the tolerance zone didn't elongate just because it was a slot; the tolerance zone was still a circle!

FRANK SNOWDEN-BRUBAKER

They would spell out inspection instructions in note form instead of using the symbols they were supposed to use. They would state, "Holes A-B need to be positioned within 0.010 of each other." Anyone in the business should know this is very wrong.

But my bottom line is this: When you look at these companies that are in a position to do the right thing and either choose not to because it will cost too much or take liberties because they don't quite understand (like the company mentioned above) or whatever the issue, then who can you really point your finger at? The pitiable inspector that has to do the bosses' bidding for fear of being replaced? Or the companies that make it clear to the inspectors to do what they're told or they will be replaced by someone who will cooperate and be a team player?

CHAPTER 1

We're Goin' to Happyland!

Roller Coaster Malfunctions Again

(Saturday, May 29, 1999)—At a popular theme park in Anytown, USA, 26 people were left stranded for up to four hours after the roller coaster stalled. Firefighters were called to the park and used cherry pickers to rescue the riders. There were no injuries.

The coaster train came to rest in the same area of track where it stopped in a similar incident on April 7.

The ride passed one inspection on April 1, and another before it re-opened after last month's mishap. Park officials say that the ride will remain closed until it passes another inspection. (www.RideAccidents.com)

Roller Coaster Fails in Illinois; Riders Stranded Upside Down for Hours

(Saturday, April 18, 1998)—At an amusement park in Anywhere, USA, 23 riders on a roller coaster were left stranded upside-down after the train in which they were riding stopped in the middle of a vertical loop. Firefighters used a cherry picker to bring the passengers to safety. Some riders were stuck for nearly three hours. Four passengers were treated at local hospitals and released.

Investigators concluded that the accident was caused by mechanical failure. The accident happened when a wheel that runs along the inside of the track broke off from the axle of the last car after a nut loosened. The ride's safety systems engaged, preventing the train from derailing.

The park has installed a new safety mechanism to the trains.

In 1986, 3 people were killed when a similar malfunction on a roller coaster in Canada caused a coaster train to derail. (www.RideAccidents.com)

My Story

THAT MORNING AT work was a little surreal. I kept trying to meet people in the eyes with a knowing glance and a nod to see if they might be thinking the same thing I was: "Do you suppose that was one of our parts?"

The year was 1999. There was a story on the evening news the previous night about how several patrons at a popular, world-recognized amusement park had to be rescued from a roller coaster via a cherry picker crane. The coaster had automatically stopped during a corkscrew loop section because a wheel fell off, leaving the riders upside down, strapped in their seats.

I was working in a machine shop where we made "tight tolerance" parts. *This* park was one of our customers, along with the DOD (Department of Defense) and other companies that required a high degree of precision in their parts.

So, how could this possibly happen? How could a wheel fall off? All the parts were made to the tightest tolerance you can imagine. A natural instinct would be to assume that it probably wasn't being maintained properly. "If you don't keep the wheels greased, they will wear out." But there are other scenarios. One that gets discarded once you verify that all the parts were certified just like they were supposed to be. And that is, the failed parts were not in tolerance to start off with. They were sold with upper management not only knowing they were out but they also wanted to "aid" in the decision if they were going to ship or not.

I know that sounds accusatory and unlikely, but these tolerances get so crazy that nonengineers (upper management) just can't believe that they really need to be held that tight. They think there may be some wiggle room they can get away with. Please allow me to offer a quick tutorial so that the average person can better understand what it takes to make the wheels turn. Bear with me—I don't want to lose anyone thinking this is getting too technical.

A human hair is approximately four-thousandths of an inch thick, or 0.004". (Imagine a comma instead of a decimal point in front of the numbers, so 0.153" is read as "153-thousandths," 0.077" is "seventy-seven-thousandths," and 0.004" is "four-thousandths" of an inch.)

A typical tight tolerance on a blueprint is +/- (plus or minus) 0.005", about the thickness of two human hairs side by side. An even tighter tolerance for special assembly requirements is +0.0000/-0.0002", read as "two-tenths" (two ten-thousandths of an inch). This is used, for instance, on press fit assemblies, like a wheel bearing on a roller coaster. The receiving hole and the mating part are so close to the same size that it is referred to as an interference fit. A special machine is used to press the parts together. Imagine drilling a hole in a block of steel so precise that it cannot vary more than a human hair split in half four times. Go ahead; I'll wait.

Not only are there machines capable of holding these tolerances, but there are inspection devices capable of measuring these parts. (More technical stuff: measurement instruments *should* be ten times more accurate than whatever they are measuring.) Seriously.

So maybe it's easier to understand when an executive makes the decision to ship parts that are out of tolerance by no more than a human hair split in half only twice. How can that possibly make any difference? Well, if the hole is too small, the bearings may grind together and wear out prematurely. If the hole is too big, the bearing can come lose and just fall out.

Now, what happens in the machine shop when a critical dimension like this gets out of tolerance? Obviously, the part should get scrapped or, if possible, reworked until it is in tolerance.

That being said, what do you suppose happens when multiple parts, fifty or a hundred, get ran before the operator or an inspector catches it? Do you think all those parts get scrapped and they just start over again? Not likely. What should happen is, the parts get quarantined, and a deviation request is sent to the customer's quality assurance or engineering department to see if maybe they can still be used. Depending on the severity of the nonconformance, the parts just may be good enough to use as is. The only other possibility is, the customer says no.

Now imagine a meeting taking place at the machine shop between the QA manager (quality assurance) and the production foreman discussing how this happened in the first place, how to prevent it from happening in the future, and what to do with all these scrap parts.

Everyone needs to understand it is critical for all parties involved that these parts get through the process as quickly as possible. The manufacturer doesn't want to be late with their delivery—that would be a mark on their performance, which could affect future orders and their bottom line. (There also might be verbiage in the contract, including fines if you are late.) The customer that assembles the components doesn't want the parts to be late either. This can cause a temporary shutdown of the assembly line (hence the fine), people getting laid off, etc. The company that sells the roller coaster doesn't want any holdups. If they have a promised delivery date, then no matter what it takes, they want to make that date. And finally, the amusement park that promised its patrons that "by the fourth of July, the biggest, baddest roller coaster to date will be ready for operation."

So now a decision has to be made: Do we submit a request for deviation and risk them rejecting the parts, which will force us to start over from scratch? And, even if they allow it, run the risk of them reevaluating us as a supplier? Or do we make a command decision, ship the parts, and hope they don't catch it?

This can be catastrophic to your reputation if they *do* catch it or even if they *don't* catch it and the parts fail. And the only other choice will be to scrap out all the bad parts, start over, and tell them that their parts are going to be late.

The cost of remaking these parts can be phenomenal. Just the machine time can be upward of fifty dollars an hour. The machinist's/operator's time is at least twenty dollars to thirty-five dollars an hour. The cost of the material will double and then you have to deal with all that scrap material. Not much room left for a profit margin.

Now let's get down to the human side of things, specifically the inspector. The inspectors are employed by people interested in making a profit. If an inspector rejects a part, then that costs everybody. Obviously, even the executives want to know that they have a competent inspector that can catch all the nonconformities that may arise in the shop. But sometimes, someone higher up wants to get involved and be the one to decide whether to ship or not.

So it helps if the inspector is a team player. In this case, *team player* means maybe "to not make a big deal over it when they decide to ship the parts anyway." But more often, it's having to sign documents, like an inspection report or a certification. Being an inspector is one profession where if you are really good at your job and you stick to your principles, you may not be appreciated as much as someone who knows when to look the other way (when the boss tells you to).

During my indoctrination at this shop, I was "advised" by my fellow inspectors on how to record the dimensions that get out of tolerance. They told me, "If you have to record a number on the inspection report, the wrong number to show that it is in tolerance, just put a tiny dot in the box next to it. Not an asterisk, just something that nobody would look twice at, but you knew what it meant. That way, if the part gets rejected, you can identify it and CYA (cover your ass). So at least when management comes after you for missing it, you can tell them, "This is one of those dimensions you told me to record as 'in tolerance.'"

OK, now for the bad part. We *did* make press fit parts, and they *did* get out of tolerance. But, these weren't parts for the roller coaster, they were for the DOD—ordnance parts, bomb components! When I rejected them, the owner tried to explain to me, to get me to understand: "They're going into a bomb! How long do they have to last?" Yes, this is an actual quote. My thought was *Until it hits the target!*

So began my brief employment at this company. Here is a short list of some of their inconsistencies:

Material Certificates

The company was required, in some cases, to use domestic materials to make the parts. All materials must be certified to guarantee points of origin and that they meet specifications. Occasionally, an order would come through, and the material cert couldn't be found. Sometimes, the supplier forgets to include it with the shipment, or it might get misplaced. Either way, a simple phone call could remedy this, unless the problem went deeper. I don't have any firsthand knowledge, but the tongue-in-cheek joke was that a little white-out and a copier work wonders. Just let it be known that you couldn't find the cert, and in a matter of minutes, one would show up! Voilà! We now had a certificate of conformance! And the inspector had to sign it with his legal signature, stating, "Yes, I am personally verifying that all the requirements have been met." This was done under duress, with the veiled threat that if you don't sign off on these parts, they will find someone who will. And in an at-will employment state, they don't need to give a reason to terminate someone.

First-Piece Verification

When a machine gets set up, the first part typically goes through a first-piece checkoff. When the setup operator finally feels comfortable, he will have another set of eyes look it over, either by another operator or by a lead person, just to make sure nothing gets missed. Everyone makes mistakes, so the thought is, with two sets of eyes, hopefully, you won't both make the same mistake. Many times, the part will also get submitted to the inspection department for a complete first-article inspection. Typically, this is reinspecting everything already checked, plus the more difficult dimensions that require a higher level of expertise or more accurate equipment.

In this shop, it was common for an inspection form to be completed by the operator and then submitted with the part to inspection for verification. However, this was just a formality the operators performed. More often than not, very little inspection was performed by the operator, but merely the spaces were filled in with numbers to show everything was in tolerance. The owner was OK with this because he knew the inspectors were going to check the part completely and that we would catch any discrepancies.

This might sound crazy, but what was even more crazy was that the majority of the workforce were his friends and relatives from his home country, his home village. During a conversation I had with him, he told me that he was obligated to give back to those who helped raise him after he was orphaned. So he brought over those same persons (or their offspring) to give them the opportunity to make a better life for themselves. No experience, very little training, and no expectations to do anything other than keep the machines running. Many of the machine operators were his extended family.

Usually the first-article parts were really close, like what you would expect, with minimal adjustments necessary. But every once in a while, you would get one where a dimension like a hole diameter was way off (supposed to be five-eighths diameter and they used a one-half-inch drill), which was obviously not even measured.

Our Foreman

One day, the shop foreman brought in some parts and told us they were "hot" to ship. When I looked over the job order, I noticed that they hadn't been passivated yet. This was a cleaning operation. In this case, there was a note on the print that stated it required a twenty-four-hour salt bath. This shop happened to be equipped with a small lab capable of performing this operation, so he grabbed the parts back and, about twenty minutes later, returned with them, still dripping wet, and stated they were now ready to ship.

Another time, we were running a part from a family of very similar parts. They all had tapped holes in each of the four corners. Some went all the way through the part, and others were tapped only partway through from each side. When we caught the mix-up (the threads did not go through), the foreman took the parts back and "fixed" them. He was excited to show us that if you are very careful and go slowly, you can match up the threads to the other side. And he was being serious! If you think about it, you have a "one in 360 degrees" chance of the threads lining up. Otherwise, you're just "cross-threading," or destroying the threads.

Our VP

The vice president once came into the inspection office and asked about a part, how much work had been performed on it so far. He was told that it had just barely gotten started. He then picked up the phone and began explaining to the customer that we had almost completed the part. Unfortunately for him, the customer told him they would take the part as is and that we could bill them for the work performed. I don't know how he talked his way out of that one. Probably told them there was a mix-up, some confusion.

Another military part had a specific cleaning operation required called liquid honing. This was needed to ensure proper adhesion of the paint. They also had a paint room and decided that the parts didn't need to be liquid honed, that it wasn't necessary. When the job came around for me to inspect, I tried to find where we had sent the parts in the past. The other inspectors were reluctant to offer an outside-service location but instead told me to check with the last person who signed off on it. This was the person whom I replaced and who was now the vice president of the company.

I asked him where I should send the parts, and he told me, "Oh, that. That's one of those things that we say we do but we don't do. Do you have a problem with that?" He said it not threateningly, or with any attitude, but more like he was concerned that I was onboard with it (that I was going to be a team player.)

Now you may be thinking, *Oh, this can't be true. This is just a disgruntled employee.* Well, you're right. I am a disgruntled employee. And stuff like this is how I got that way.

Anyway, I answered his question, "Yes, I have a problem with that! I'm not going to sign my name to something that we don't do!" And I got up and walked out of his office.

A couple of minutes later, he called me back into his office. He wanted to explain the situation: "The part doesn't need liquid honing," he said. "The paint will stick just fine. But if we try to get them to change their print, it would cost them a lot of money. Do you have any idea how many copies of this print are floating around the country that they would need to change?"

I responded, "Oh, you're trying to save them money?"

"Yes," he said.

"So," I asked, "do you charge them for it?"

There was a long-enough pause that I didn't wait around for an answer. I just turned on my heel and walked out of his office. Soon after that meeting, I handed in my two-week notice.

CHAPTER 2

Foundry Life

D URING THE HOUSING-AND-LOAN-CAUSED recession, I found myself taking a job in a foundry. Work was scarce, and positions were cut. Foundry work is "something no one strives toward." This was a quote from a former boss who also got caught in the crunch and had to settle for a foundry job.

Towards the end of the first decade in 2000, I worked as the quality assurance manager in a foundry. (While there, I wrote their ISO manual, cover-to-cover in eleven months. You would be hard-pressed to find a handful of companies that can make that claim.) It was an extremely filthy building because they worked with sand-cast molds. The air was constantly filled with this black dust mostly comprised of silica, a very fine medium found in the sand used to make the molds. There is even a medical condition caused by breathing in silica called silicosis: "a lung disease caused by prolonged inhalation of dust containing silica and marked by the development of fibrous tissue in the lungs and a resultant chronic shortness of breath" (Encarta Dictionary).

I was diagnosed with possibly having silicosis when I had undergone an MRI for what was found to be pneumonia. While reading my results, the doctor noted some mysterious clouding in my lungs and asked if I had ever worked in a foundry. When I told her I did, she gave me some literature about silicosis. After that visit, I always wore my mask.

Getting back on topic, this foundry dealt with exotic metals that were very durable under extreme conditions. Several of their contracts were with pipeline manufacturers. We made components that, in turn, would be machined into valve mechanisms. Yes, valves in oil pipelines. I was told by the CEO that the materials used were so expensive that even before it was poured into a mold, it was worth "as much as your car" (about five thousand dollars). We would pour it into a mold, clean it up, grind off the rough edges, and send it to a machine shop, where it would get about eight hours of machining to fabricate the end product: one side—one-half of a valve housing.

So you can see how expensive this is getting. And each part is only about eight to twelve inches thick, for each half. Maybe two feet thick at the most just for the valve of a pipeline, which could be hundreds of miles long.

You don't have to imagine the environmental implications if one of these valves would fail in the field. They have. I'm not saying these specific valves, just valves in general.

Toward the end of my employment, the company landed a contract that specifically stated that no weld repairs were to be allowed on any of their parts. This was a tall order since there were very few instances where at least some repairs weren't performed on the casts. It was just a matter of fact—a part of the process. There was an operation dedicated to this because there was almost always some form of void caused by gasses or dirt or some foreign particulates that get into the part. This, in turn, needed to be dug out with grinders and weld-repaired.

So you can imagine the customer bragging about how his parts are completely solid with no weld repairs. The perception by your average layperson being that welds could break loose, chip, or cause stress fractures or any of a number of issues that he might think are possibilities. Well, I'm not a metallurgist or an engineer. Maybe the weld repairs do cause weak points, but that's not even the point here. The point is, the customer was paying for weld-free parts, and that's what they were expecting.

In an e-mail conversation between our CEO and the middleman that forwarded us the job, my boss, the CEO was lamenting on how impossibly high the cost would soar if they had to keep scrapping out and remaking the parts until they had a perfect part with no weld repairs. The response from the middleman was to do whatever we needed "to keep the lights on."

On the very first round, there was a bad incident with one of the pours. A small piece of the upper mold broke loose and caused a depression on the surface of the part. This needed a weld repair larger than any I had seen before. The equivalent volume of a person's hand had to be filled in with a puddle of weld material. In this circumstance, this repair really could have been an issue with the performance of the final product.

My signature was needed on the certificate of conformance. Suffice it to say, I did not sign the COC and was gone from the company before the parts shipped.

In a letter of recommendation, the CEO wrote, "[My name] cut our in-house scrap rate in half, resulting in higher profits, so [company name] could finally purchase a new induction furnace, which was necessary for our survival."

This letter was written after I quit. I told the newly hired President, "F'-you! I quit!" after he rushed me from his chair and stopped about 8 inches from my face, yelling at me. I didn't turn in a two-week notice; I just walked out the door. There were a lot of hostilities, but I think the CEO might have been a little concerned about what I might say or do after I left.

He even told unemployment that I was laid off so that I wouldn't be so desperate financially.

Not the First Time

The first foundry that I worked in was an aluminum foundry in the late eighties. It was a small shop, with no real automation. The workers would dip a ladle into a pool of molten aluminum and pour it into a press mold, which was at an elevated height that they had to reach up to. To say the conditions were ungodly would be accurate. The temperatures at the presses were always well over one hundred degrees. The operators would bring in their own coolers full of ice water to dump over their heads to avoid heatstroke.

So they would pour in the aluminum and wait the required length of time. The press would then be opened and the mold removed by hand wearing a thick cloth glove. Then the surfaces of the die would be sprayed with an antistick substance, closed, and the process would be repeated for the length of their shift.

One of the parts they ran was a DOD part called a slider. This was a small part that was assembled into a grenade (yes, another ordnance part). It was supposed to slide over to arm the grenade after a different mechanism activated it.

Well, the parts got rejected from the DOD due to a problem caused by a burr called flash. Flash is caused by a slight misalignment at the point where the aluminum enters the pocket for each part. This is very common and very difficult to avoid, so it is typically dealt with afterward. The flash was causing the slider to stick, and consequently, the grenade wouldn't arm.

The company needed to come up with a method to make the parts acceptable. Removing the flash was going to be very costly. This cost could not be added to the price of the product; that's not how the government works. They had already won the contract with their bid and were stuck in an agreement that would end up making very little profit or even costing them money.

The QA manager came up with a method to smash the flash down onto the surface of the part. He was hoping that this would be acceptable because, technically, it was now dimensionally in tolerance (it measured correctly). But now instead of removing or eliminating the problem, he just turned it into a different problem. There was no guarantee that these smashed pieces of flash wouldn't break loose and again cause problems with how the grenade functioned or if the DOD would accept his method of dealing with the flash. Just because they measured in tolerance didn't excuse the fact that it was an attribute that was not supposed to be there.

I could see the writing on the wall and turned in my two-week notice slightly after that decision. My boss likened me to a "rat leaving a sinking ship." Yes, he actually spoke those words. I told him he could stay on this sinking ship if he wanted, but I wasn't going down with it.

The last foundry I worked at was also short-lived. I was hired as a temp and didn't stay long enough to get hired on.

The only issue I had with them was a recurring issue that I've witnessed throughout my career. That is, "How deeply should you investigate when you find nonconformances during inspections?" To me, this seems obvious, but again, upper management doesn't want to invest any more time or energy into anything that they think they can get away with. Just one example, and I'll move on.

The part I was checking was a lid for a container. It was about two feet in diameter and somewhat heavy and difficult to handle. There were only twenty-four parts in the order in two containers. The inspection plan required two pieces from each container for a spot inspection. I found a reject part in one container and decided that the entire order should be sorted.

My boss interjected and decided that since I only found one reject in one of the boxes, then only that box needed to be sorted. My thought process was that since I found one reject and the order was for only twenty-four parts, then the possibility of another reject was greater than the time you might spend wasting to ensure the rest of the parts were good. Why take the chance? Because ignorance is bliss?

FRANK SNOWDEN-BRUBAKER

CHAPTER 3

The Early Years

WORKING AS AN inspector in the machining industry can be very unstable, at least in my experience. No company wants to hire a person whose only job is to tell them if their parts are good or not. It would be much more efficient and cost-effective if the operators could just monitor themselves, inspect their own work, and cut out this excess baggage. My running gag, when someone would ask what I do for a living, is to say "I don't *do* anything. I just look at what other people do."

But this position is more customer driven. The customer needs to know there is a check-and-balance system in place, so there is no conflict of interests. You don't want the person who makes the parts to be the same person responsible for policing himself. How many of us could be completely honest where, if you run bad parts, it could cost you your job—or at least affect your next raise or any advancement opportunities?

The inspector is more of a necessary evil, like internal affairs in a police department. IA always seems to be viewed as the bad guys, trying to catch a would-be-honest cop who, in turn, is just trying to do *his* job the best he can. In machining, that may be an operator that tends to run parts out of tolerance, and it's the inspector's job to try to keep bad parts from exiting the building. And if the operator keeps getting caught, he may get replaced.

So the inspector is treated like the bad guy. Instead of being appreciated for making sure that bad parts don't go out the door and get rejected by the customer, he is treated like someone who is just trying to find mistakes being made by his fellow employees.

In one of my earliest jobs in machining, I realized my calling and was made an in-process inspector. I was just a machine operator myself, being trained in to set up automatic screw machines. But the foreman saw something in me that he thought would pan out into something bigger. It was the quality of my parts. Every time he came by to check on me, they were always in tolerance, near perfect.

So he offered me the option: along with keeping all six of my machines running, I could be the roving inspector. And so started my career as an inspector!

This was fine with me. Once I loaded my machines, they would run themselves. I would start 'em up, tweak anything that needed adjusting, and then just keep loading them with material, making periodic adjustments when needed. I had them all timed out, so I knew exactly when one needed to get reloaded. I compared it to a juggler with spinning plates on top of sticks. This might be lost on some younger readers. It was an act you might see on *The Ed Sullivan Show* . . . oh, never mind. Once I had them all humming, I would start my rounds.

During one of my rounds, I approached one of the younger operators. This kid had a real attitude toward me and the position. I came up to him, and he proceeded to hand me a part that he was saving for me. That's not how it's done. That would defeat the purpose if I just inspect a part that he'd already inspected. But I accepted it with the knowledge that after I checked that part, I'd just grab the next one that he ran or whichever one I decided to check.

So I started my inspection, and guess what. The part that he was saving for me was out! It was an axle shaft that had a tight tolerance outside diameter (another one of those press fit dimensions). And using a very sensitive micrometer called a pressure mic, it was clear that the diameter was out of tolerance!

So what do you suppose happened to him for running bad parts? Not a thing. "These things happen. It could happen to anyone," the foreman told me. But here is where it takes a weird twist. I was brought into his office, and he explained to me that I had gotten too much joy out of finding the problem. No kidding. This is how inspectors are treated.

Now if I had started hooting and jumping up and down, shouting how this little punk ran a bunch of bad parts, then I could have understood being reprimanded for acting improperly. But all I did was

FRANK SNOWDEN-BRUBAKER

smirk at the fact that this stupid kid with the bad attitude toward me couldn't even make sure his sample was in tolerance!

But that is how inspectors are treated. We are told to be careful about how we talk to the operators, not to hurt their feelings—"No one wants to be told they are running bad parts." So I always had to tiptoe around and talk apologetically when I found nonconforming features while doing my inspections.

On my first job in machining, I didn't have one single tool. I remember, after my first paycheck and a visit from the *Snap-on* guy, I purchased my first tools ever: a pliers and a flathead screwdriver! It was fun and exciting realizing that I might have found something that I thought I was good at and liked doing for a living!

A couple of days later, one of the guys brought in a beat-up old tackle box. He said that I could have it to keep my new tools in. It was kind of a joke, kind of a jab, but I loved it. I was one happy rookie. (I still have that box.)

Way back then, people didn't care as much that every little thing had to be in spec. We operated more on the three *F*s: fit, form, and function. Will it go together? Does it look good? And will it work? What else mattered, right? Who cared if a dimension got a little out of tolerance! If it worked, it worked! If that sounds familiar, then you're paying attention. It bears repeating.

I even worked in a shop where a majority of their parts didn't have any blueprints. All they had was a pegboard wall of sample parts. The idea was to make the part like the sample. There was no tolerance or spec we had to hold it to; just "make it like the sample." A tolerance comparison was either a blond hair, a redhead, or a pubic. And without getting too politically incorrect, things were a lot more sexist and racist forty years ago. Sorry, that's just the way things were. I remember having to take down a sexually explicit calendar because a customer was coming through the shop for a tour and there was going to be a woman with them.

Those days are long gone. Now most parts are held to the utmost scrutiny. There are no parts that can go through any shop without some form of inspection.

Going back even further, "Just push it down flat on this surface here, and turn the screw until the dial goes to zero!"

That was all the training I needed for my first exposure as an inspector. I was barely eighteen and a torpedoman in the navy. They had me climb up into a torpedo tube on a submarine to align the guide rollers.

No experience. Never before saw the dial instrument I was now qualified to operate (it's called a drop indicator.) And yes, they shut the hatch on me and pretended to launch me, but that's another story.

Other duties I was entrusted with was inspecting all the tools used in the torpedo shop and the equipment used for "weapons moves." This included hoists, come-alongs and cranes, torpedo straps (like the yellow tow straps used for towing cars), and what we called bomb carts. These were used to move torpedoes along the deck after they were raised from the torpedo shop. We would set the torpedo on the cart and roll it to the other end of the ship, where it would be lowered onto the submarine.

I was also assigned to inspect some aspects of the infrastructure of the ship, including hatches and emergency drains.

My inspections of the tools were unremarkable. Everything worked—no frayed wires, faulty switches, etc. Sometimes, the torpedo straps would show signs of wear, and they would be replaced. The hoists and cranes always checked fine, and the bomb carts required little maintenance—they were similar to a little red wagon.

But when it came to the ship's integrity, this is where it took a hard left turn: There were multiple hatches throughout the torpedo decks that were supposed to get routine inspections to ensure they closed completely. They had to be watertight (for obvious reasons).

When I was assigned to inspect them, I started discovering that some of the deck hatches wouldn't seal completely. They were mainly the hatches we would raise and lower torpedoes through. They were somewhat long, and this was probably why it was difficult to get a good seal. Nonetheless, they didn't seal—they were not watertight, and they got put on the to-do list.

The other issue I discovered was that several of the emergency drains throughout the shop wouldn't open. Over the years of nonuse (and not getting inspected) they were corroded, rusted, and ended up getting painted shut. This got the attention of some higher-ups as a more serious issue that needed to be dealt with immediately.

I tried in vain to pry them open with a come-along we had in the shop. It wasn't cutting it, wasn't big enough. I managed to acquire a six-ton come-along from a friend who worked in the engine rooms. I originally wanted to borrow one. They had dozens of them. But he told me, with a nod and a wink, that he couldn't loan it out. So I read between the lines and placed one at the bottom of an emergency-escape hatch and tied a rope to it. Then I left the area by standard means, went to the top of the escape hatch, and raised the hoist up by the rope. It felt like I was on a covert mission, sneaking through the decks with a six-ton come-along over my shoulder. We snipped off their ID tag and made up our own and affixed it to our new come-along for the torpedo shop.

Now we could muscle the drain covers loose and break through the years of layers of paint and neglect.

The following are excerpts from my evaluation: "During this marking period TMSN [my name] has been assigned to many tasks that would normally be performed by a petty officer. He has accepted these tasks readily and demonstrated his ability to work on his own to complete a job in an orderly and competent manner. . . . By utilizing personal friendships throughout the command, TMSN [my name] has been able to get shop and divisional assistance to correct problems that normally would have been very time consuming."

These comments are directly related to what I have just been describing.

As you can surmise, I am not one to shirk my duties. I am a perfectionist, which is probably a good trait to have in an inspector. Obviously, my predecessors did not perform their duties as required, but I am not like that. I tend to take things to the nth degree (that's why I've had twenty-three jobs in thirty-five years).

CHAPTER 4

Taking Extraordinary Means

THE FIRST TIME I went to seek help outside of the normal venues was when I was working in a precious metal plating lab in the late eighties. The two main precious metals being gold and silver, and then a few other undercoatings that were needed to help the other metals adhere to the surfaces better (and possibly for other reasons, but I'm not a metallurgist).

One of their customers was, again, the US government and, more specifically, the DOD. I'll just refer to a few parts that we plated. One was a component of a land mine called a Bouncing Betty, and the other two went into satellites.

The Bouncing Betty component was a block of steel that received a coating process called electroless nickel plating (everything else was called electroplating.) Electroless plating is a method where the part is simply submerged into the plating bath for a predetermined time. The expectation is that when it is removed, it will have the correct amount of plating on it.

One drawback of this process is that if you pull the parts early and they don't have enough plating on them, you can't return them to the bath and just add more—it won't adhere. So to avoid this, you include samples with the parts—"coupons" of the same type of material that you can pull and measure at different intervals.

I think you know where I'm headed with this. Sometimes, they would pull the part early and then re-submerge them in an attempt to add more plating. When you do that, the plating can be checked with a tape test. A specific type of tape placed on the surface and then quickly removed will detach any plating that was added.

Do you think they ever tried to sneak bad parts through? Maybe brought me a sample from a lot that they didn't double dip so that I wouldn't catch it? And do you suppose the customer might do their own tape test since it is so easy and inexpensive to perform?

(At one point, they actually posted a notice by the time clock that read: "While OSHA [Occupational Safety and Health Administration] is conducting their inspection, do not dump any sulfuric acid down the sewer drains." They even forgot to take down the notice while OSHA was there performing their inspections!)

Moving along, another one of their parts was a sheet of electrical circuitry that was going into satellites. These were going to be exposed to extreme conditions, so it was vital that they be protected from the elements. We coated them with 99.9 percent pure gold. Or at least that's what the certificate of conformance stated.

There were many times when I inspected these sheets where I could see with the unaided, naked eye the color differences when the gold in the plating tanks got low. It started to look more brown than gold.

I even overheard the platers on different occasions complaining that "[the owner] was so cheap that he wouldn't replace or add to the bath until [the gold] was almost completely [depleted]."

So how could these parts pass an inspection? We had an x-ray machine that could measure the thickness of every layer of metal plating on the parts. I would set the sheet over a small window on the top of the unit and push the start button (now I'm wondering if I might have been exposed to x-ray radiation), and the readings would appear on a screen. I was instructed that whenever there was a result that was out of tolerance, I was to push the Delete button, move the sample around a little, and take another reading until I got all good readings for my report.

This was one of the more blatantly obvious nonconformances. Another part we plated was a small pin, about the thickness of a paper clip and approximately an inch and a half long. It ended up with a wide range of plating thicknesses due to the process. They were loaded into a plastic barrel with a screen-like surface that allowed the plating material to pass through and coat the objects inside.

To cut costs, they would put as many pins as possible into the barrel. It doesn't take a rocket scientist (or a metallurgist) to see that the pins closer to the outer surface will get more plating and the pins at the center will get less. So the outer pins were over plated, and the inner pins were under plated.

Many times, plating tolerance is worded as a minimum thickness, so over plating is rarely a rejectable condition. But obviously, a company doesn't want to waste money or materials, so an effort is always made to meet the minimum requirements.

The problem was that the inner pins ended up being under plated. Without enough protective coating, the pins could fall subject to the elements and rust or corrode and possibly fail.

Then the last straw. One day, I came in to work to find my signature on a certificate of conformance in my boss's handwriting! He didn't try to forge my signature; he just signed my name with his handwriting!

That was when I decided to take action against what I considered to be a mind-set of disregard that was consuming the industry.

I didn't know whom to turn to. I tried claiming to unemployment that I was a whistle-blower, but I didn't fit the definition. I hadn't been fired for making provable accusations/claims. I didn't have a list of improprieties performed by the company. It was looking like I had to start recording and categorizing, with dates and times of when and to what degree the improprieties were committed, if I wanted to go this route. And I would have to get fired for it.

I don't recall how I got hooked up with the person I dubbed as *The Equalizer* (a popular TV series in the late eighties). He said he was an ex-navy, ex-CIA operative who was now in a position to look into claims like mine.

Things were finally looking up. I now had an ally that I could go to with all the issues that I've been dealing with. My voice was finally going to be heard. I was ready to go after these businesses that I felt were acting with disregard to legal contracts and ultimately could be putting peoples' lives at stake (or at least providing components that were misrepresented and could fail).

So began the investigation. I explained to him about how the gold plating was thin and impure, how the silver-coated parts were under plated, and how my signature was forged on a cert by the president. In fact, I had so many things I reported to him that I think he started to doubt that what I said was completely true or maybe an exaggeration—you know, the "disgruntled employee" assumption.

Anyway, "the equalizer" was directing his investigation toward me first. He said he wanted to eliminate the possibility of false claims, which was fine, except he never seemed to want to turn the corner and at least start looking at the things I reported to him.

So that was a dead end. I couldn't believe it! I just couldn't find anyone that would listen to me, give me the benefit of a doubt.

They ended up firing me shortly after hiring a cute little thing barely out of high school. (The guys in the shop were openly hitting on her right away.) Anyway, he said that they couldn't afford me. Like I said, in an at-will employment state, they don't need to give a reason to fire you.

CHAPTER 5

Bring in the FBI

F AST-FORWARD A COUPLE years, I was getting interviewed by a guy whom I thought looked like a character from the movie *Casino*. Joe Pesci's "Nicky Santoro," to be exact—all the way from the gold necklace with the Italian good-luck charm and the bejeweled fingers to the cocky attitude. During the interview, he explained, "This is a surplus-supply depot. All the parts are overruns and were already inspected, so reinspecting them was [redundant]. But we tell our customers that we perform a certain level of auditing to make sure the parts were correct." He explained, "The criteria might say that you need to check a certain percentage of parts, so out of a hundred parts, you might need to inspect fifteen. So what *we* do is, you inspect a few key features on a couple of parts—you know, make sure the threads are good, check a tight-tolerance diameter, and then eyeball a few more just to make sure there aren't any obvious defects on them. After that, fill out the inspection form, saying you did the required amount."

I know; unbelievable, right? I wasn't even hired yet, and he was laying all his cards on the table!

That was on a Friday, and I was destitute because I just couldn't hold a job (with my high moral standards and all), so I accepted it. That weekend, I did some soul-searching, and when Monday rolled around, I called to tell him that I changed my mind.

Believe it or not, that wasn't the first or last time an interviewer showed his hand to me before I was even hired.

It had now gotten to the point where I would flat out tell a prospective employer during the interview, "If you're just looking for a yes-man, then please don't even consider me. But if you want accurate measurements of the products, then I am your man."

I had used that line during the interview at a company where I was working in the late '90s. The foreman told me in a disgusted tone that they were not one of those places. Yeah right.

It was after I was fired from there that I went to the Feds.

In my experiences over the years, I have gotten along just fine with the good operators and the ones that at least try to be good at their jobs. But I have little patience for the operators or machinists (or management) who put quality second to quantity because they are too focused on making their rate or a ship date (or profits).

On my first week there, I had rejected a part back to the floor. The part was called a bezel. An example would be the frame around the monitor on an old-fashioned TV screen or, in this case, an airport radar monitor. The print called out a maximum radius for the corners. These were oversized and needed to be ground to make them sharper. A few minutes after I rejected them, a barrel-chested large man in a suit came into the inspection office, carrying the bezel. "Did you reject this?" he said, looking at me.

I replied simply, "Yes."

"Well, you need to understand, they have to use a Dremel to make that radius. They gotta grind it out by hand, and it's really hard to get it perfect."

I just stared out at him like I didn't care what difficulties they had in order to make it right and responded with a drawn-out deadpan "Oh."

Then he went on, "So what does it measure?"

I told him, "It's over the maximum. I didn't think you wanted me to spend too much time on it, but if you want, I can get some exact numbers," again with my screw-you tone.

He saw that I wasn't going to be bullied and left in a huff. "Who the hell was that?" I asked the other inspectors.

"*That* was the president, the owner's son," they told me.

Oh boy, off to a great start!

This place had a running gag because of how the owner and management were running it into the ground. The company was built by the father, and after a court decision, the wife got the company and put her boys in charge. They never had to learn anything about the business; they just had to run it. The gag was a lament by the brothers: when something didn't go right, they tended to say "How do these things keep happening?"

One example of this was when they would send parts out to get them heat-treated, a process of hardening the parts after machining. The parts would come back warped, and they would say "How do these things keep happening?"

"Because you don't learn from your mistakes, because you don't want to hire somebody who understands heat treating and how to avoid these things from happening!"

I would sometimes call customer engineering departments to discuss discrepancies with the blueprints. (I am going to venture into that unbelievable area again.) Many times, there would be callouts on their prints that were in error. I don't want to name companies, but let's just say that almost every company had some form of issues with its prints, which, again, is pretty scary.

The barrel-chested brother caught wind of this and promptly put a stop to it. He approached me, saying, "It's not your job to correct their prints for them!"

To that, I responded, "What if they sent you a print that said to drill a one-inch hole through a one-inch piece of stock?"

He said, "I'd send them a box of chips!"

I had gotten a reputation for being a little overconfident in my attitude (personally, I think my attitude matched my abilities quite well). We joked around in inspection as much as we could to break the tension. One of the gags I used to say was "Sure, I make mistakes too. But you better bring a camera and mark it on the calendar, 'cause they are few and far between."

One day, a foreman carried into inspection a component for a ventilating system in a new-development military tank, which was still a prototype, called the Excalibur.

When he brought in the part, he said, "Here you go. This one's got your name on it."

The part was a welded-up section of the aforementioned vent with a five-sided, base-mounting bracket that morphed from an irregular polygon into a polyhedron, into a cylinder, made a right angle turn, and then morphed again into a parallelogram that tilted about forty-five degrees and ended up facing ninety degrees from the base. (Sorry, I was just having a little fun with you.) The bolt patterns for both mounting surfaces had to correlate with each other so that it would assemble. Let's just say it was complicated.

Now, it wouldn't be such a big deal to inspect if you have the right equipment. But when all you have is a tape measure and a square . . . (You wouldn't believe all the times I've heard the words "Just do the best you can with what we have," or maybe you would after reading this book.)

Anyway, after an extensive examination, I concluded that the part was not in tolerance. I rejected it back to production, and about five minutes later, this rough-around-the-edges gentleman came into inspection, looked at me, and asked, "Did you reject that part?"

I told him I did, and he said, "I tried to tell them their lame-ass fixture wasn't going to work!" Then he turned and left the room.

The other inspectors stopped in their tracks in awe of what just happened. They both said to me, "That was the closest thing to a compliment that guy has ever given anyone!" He was their lead welder and had been there for years.

Production kept trying to get the part right, but then the government cancelled the order. Hell, they cancelled the tank!

This place had a habit of screwing stuff up and then just trying to cover it up. And when they did, they usually brought their screw-ups into the inspection room and "fixed" them in there. I think just because it was a somewhat large room with extra space to move around and because it was clean and quiet and carpeted and away from the chaos out on the production floor.

One time, they brought in a part that had a special-colored plating. They had to do some more machining to it after plating, and when they did, they chipped it. So they brought the part into inspection and painted over the areas where the protective coating was missing.

I remember scolding them not to do that stuff in there because "I need deniability! Now I am an accomplice, a coconspirator!"

Another example of that still haunts me today. We were performing the final inspections on a cabinet-type part for the aviation department, a console for a part I mentioned earlier, the airport-radar-monitor housing. There was the box housing, a drawer, and multiple components that were needed to construct the unit. After it was completely assembled, one of the other inspectors was giving it a final visual, and that was when he noticed that the box housing was missing some plating in a somewhat large area in an inside corner. It looked like when they submerged it, they didn't rotate the part to allow a bubble to escape. So how do you suppose they addressed it? Did they call the customer to see what type of repair might be allowed? Did they call the platers to see what they could do? No, they went down to the nearest hardware store and bought a can of spray paint and just touched it up themselves. I remember the conversation between the brothers:

"What do you think we should do?"

"I don't know. The parts are already late, and the source inspector's gonna be here tomorrow!"

"Let's just cover it up with spray paint, and if they catch it, we'll tell them that the parts came in that way."

Yup, that's how these brothers worked. So when the source inspector showed up . . . By the way, a "source inspector" is an inspector from the customer you are selling the parts to. They come out to us, the source, and do the inspection here so that a lot of time isn't wasted shipping bad parts back and forth.

Anyway, when the source inspector caught the repair job, he got very concerned about what he was seeing. I remember him questioning one of the other inspectors about it. He looked like a kid caught with his hand in the cookie jar. He told the source guy that he didn't know anything about it, as he was instructed, and "that was how we received them."

The source guy wasn't happy with his explanation and told us he was going to bring in *his* boss to take a look-see.

Now the brothers were starting to sweat. This could be a major blow, getting caught in a cover-up where they obviously bold-faced lied and tried to sneak parts through that they spray-painted.

The next morning, the source inspector showed up with his boss. He was a very pleasant fellow, putting everyone at ease with his comforting personality. Seemed he was going to get to the bottom of this so that everyone could relax and get back to business as usual.

He was using a desk about six feet from me when he called the platers. I could only hear his side of the conversation: first the inquiry, then a lot of "Oh. OK. Uh-huh. Uh-huh. No, I got it . . . Yup, thanks a lot."

He got off the phone and explained to everyone that whenever that happens, a bubble gets lodged in a part, they have a procedure where they cover that area with a special spray (paint?) that is approved by the customer (in this case, the government). So no worries. Everyone can relax.

It was everything I could do to keep my jaw from hitting the floor! This senior inspector just accepted the word of the plating shop that they were allowed to modify, alter, adjust, revise a government requirement, which was stated on a print, without getting approval first!

I couldn't believe the incompetence I had just witnessed! Not to mention the conversation at the other end. I was imagining the foreman hanging up and questioning the person whom he thought might have tried to do the cover-up at their end. Someone might have lost their job because of that. It never occurred to me that our bosses would have the foresight or courage to conspire with the platers to give them the heads-up. After all, it was the platers that they were throwing under the bus in the first place.

Try to keep in mind this is a nonfiction book. It's not a sci-fi or fantasy, and I will get to the FBI part in a minute (or two).

There were times when I would inspect a part, report my findings (quite a bit out of tolerance), and they would say, "It's just a prototype. It doesn't have to be perfect."

In my mind, a prototype should be as near perfect as possible. The whole point of making prototype parts is because they want to make sure, in the real physical world that they are going to fit up properly. So this is where the engineers will make any adjustments or revisions if the parts don't fit as planned.

One last example before I go on. One of the welders took exception to a part he had welded, and I rejected. Understandably, it was a difficult part to weld, and there were impossible tolerances he was expected to hold. But the part was out, and my findings were what they were.

He came storming into the inspection office, demanding that I pass his part—that it "will work just fine"!

This was kind of a shock to me because up to that point, we had gotten along very well. In fact, this company had a couple of extracurricular activities that we both shared—softball in the summer and wallyball (indoor volleyball) in the winter—and I thought we were, if not friends, at least on friendly terms.

I tried talking to him, telling him that the tolerances were going to be tough to hit, but he just came back with "It's not your job to hold

up these parts. It's your job to pass them and get them out the door!"
Yes, he really said that.

By now, it had turned into a shouting match, and everyone in the front office could hear the commotion. People were freaking out.

The plant manager brought me into his office to calm me down and find out what was going on. After a brief discussion, he concluded that I was not wrong to reject the parts, but I was out of line for letting it escalate the way I did. Of course, the inspector always needs to be polite and apologetic, even contrite, when reporting his findings.

I took advantage of this meeting to remind him that he was delinquent with our agreement of my pay increases when I was first hired. After looking back in his records, he agreed that yes, he was, and that he would rectify that for the next pay period. To that, I said, "No. Make it retroactive to be on this paycheck. You're already late, and there is no reason to wait any longer."

He reluctantly agreed but added, "Will this make you happy?" The obvious implication was that he thought he was buying me off to be a team player. Read "Look the other way when asked." I just answered, "It's a start."

It had now gotten to the point where I would leave blanks on the inspection reports for dimensions that were not in tolerance. Another one of the inspectors would finish filling them in. When it finally came to a head and they cut me loose, my boss tried telling unemployment that I had an attitude problem and cited the meeting we had as a warning and even mentioned the date. That made it too easy. I just showed unemployment the date that I received one of the biggest raises anyone in the company had ever received. There were other idiotic statements made by other witnesses. One brother, in a written statement, said that I "left the meeting singing John Cougar Mellencamp's "Authority Song": "I fight authority, authority always wins." That was an indictment against me? There was something else he said to me, which I included in my statement: "This is not your company. I didn't see you at the bank when the papers were signed." To which I replied, "Just because you own the company doesn't mean you can do whatever you want!"

I won the unemployment claim. They said, paraphrasing, that even though my actions might have been detrimental to the company, I was not acting out of malice (words to the effect).

OK, now I was unemployed. Now I had some time on my hands to prosecute these criminals to the full extent of the law.

I contacted the FBI and explained to them how they were systematically, repeatedly, knowingly selling inferior, defective, and possibly dangerous products to the DOD, air traffic control, and aerospace contractors.

The FBI representative asked me if I could provide them some proof, some specifics so that they could investigate my accusations. I told them that I could draw up some simulated blueprints with explanations of what the issues were for each offense.

And so started my mission. I began my furious enterprise and soon had a dozen or so drawings "with circles and arrows and a paragraph on the back of each one explaining how it would be used against [them] in a court of law" (Arlo Guthrie's "Alice's Restaurant").

When I was ready, they returned to my house, and after looking over my renderings and hearing my testimony, they decided they had enough to pursue my allegations.

There was one more technicality they had to get out of the way first. The next thing I had to do was pass a lie detector test. I was apprehensive of how I would do just because I would be stressed out and was afraid my nerves would get the best of me.

I went to the FBI building in the downtown area where I was met by my assigned agents, and escorted up to the floor where the elevator did not stop! No kidding. We had to get off on the floor below and walk up a flight of stairs to get there. This was getting serious.

They brought me into this somewhat dark room that kind of looked like an oversize storage closet. There was a person already waiting in the room—the lie detector operator or polygrapher. I was surprised to see what looked like one of those old-fashioned lie detectors I've seen in the movies (the same one that Robert De Niro's character used in *Meet the Fockers*). I asked (like the smart-ass I am), "Oh, the latest and greatest, some high-tech equipment here?" I'm sure that was the first time they ever heard that, and they were quick to point out that yes, just because it was older, it was still the best thing for detecting lies.

Before they hooked me up, they wanted to get me to relax, probably for a better baseline. They explained what they were about to do, the extent of the questions, and they asked me a couple of questions, I guess, to find out what kind of character I may have. They asked if I had ever lied to a police officer, a teacher, or maybe even a priest—you know, persons of authority. Well, yeah. I was a kid once. I wasn't exactly a juvenile delinquent, but I wasn't a saint either. That's when they started looking at each other like I just wasted a lot of their time.

So they strapped me in, wound curly wire leads around my chest, and put sensors on my fingertips. They asked me a couple of very basic baseline questions: "How old are you?" "What is your name?" "What is your street address?" and *not* things like what they show on TV like "Do you love your mother? Hate your father?" (How would they know, right?)

When they were done getting a baseline set, they asked me one question about my claims. Just one. "Is everything you told us the truth?" That's it! It was that simple. I said yes, and I passed with flying colors.

So began their investigation. I kept tabs on how they were doing. I would call once a week or so. They never seemed to be making any progress though. I even contacted a coworker from the company to ask if anything out of the ordinary was going on. He was not happy with me when he found out what I'd done. I was messing with his job, his income, his future.

After a few months of getting the runaround, they finally told me that they couldn't corroborate any of my claims. I even offered to go to the customer's shops and show them on the exact parts where they were bad. That wasn't going to happen. I could only conclude four different possibilities: (1) they were the same inspectors that missed the rejects in the first place and were trying to save their jobs, (2) the persons checking the parts were also totally incompetent, (3) they were on the take (not likely), or (4) they were protecting their fellow inspectors who originally missed it.

I guess there could have been one other possibility: all the sample parts that they inspected were good. Again, not likely.

After that fiasco, I had completely given up on trying to do the right thing. It was obvious to me that short of writing a tell-all book and exposing these companies to the world, nothing was ever going to change. In fact, unfortunately, I still feel that manufacturing will probably continue with business as usual, and I will be dismissed as a disgruntled employee, attempting shock jock methods just to sell books. Please, world, prove me wrong!

CHAPTER 6

The Medical Field

YES, LIKE IT or not, this even hemorrhages into the medical field.

As you may suspect, things are more controlled when you are making parts that are going into a human body. Just as much or more than the military. You have to show traceability for every step of the way, from the purchased materials to every instrument used during inspection of each and every part.

One of the reasons why costs get so high when you're dealing with medical parts is strictly cosmetic. I'll give you an example: In a typical household silverware drawer, you have knives, forks, spoons, etc. Each one is perfectly capable of delivering its cargo to its destination. Even if they get slightly bent over time, from scooping out ice cream or lifting a roast out of a pan, they still work just fine. They just may not nest together perfectly in the tray. Well, not so for medical instruments. We were packaging fifty or more utensils in a packet, and if they didn't line up absolutely perfectly, they were junk. Even though the tools wouldn't enter an operating room that way, they would be divvied up with multiple instruments per tray. It would be like a soup spoon on one side of the plate and a dessert spoon on the other side, completely imperceptible to anyone if there was any difference between the two. One spoon might have a slight more curve to it, so if you placed one on top of the other, "Oh my god! That won't work! They don't sit perfectly together." I know I'm getting preachy. I'll try to get over it.

That was when I worked at a machine shop where we made the parts. The bad news was when I was a receiving inspector in one of the most prestigious medical companies on the planet. Don't worry though; the parts that were supplied were always exceptional. I don't believe I ever had to reject a single one. Not one. What was bad was the quality of the inspectors they had in the receiving department. I'll set it up for you; this is what I witnessed:

There was a time when the company needed to fill a high number of inspector positions. Apparently, they figured that since the quality of the parts supplied were pretty much beyond reproach, the main requirement for the inspectors was that they could fog a mirror. And it is not a secret that companies can get away with paying women less than men. I am not being sexist or a misogynist, but I am repeating what I was told and what I witnessed. I am not saying that women are less qualified than men. What I am saying is that the receiving department at this company was a "girls' club." It was filled with under qualified inspectors that spent more time discussing *Avon* products and *Tickle Me Elmo* toys, and one person liked to polish her fingernails under a microscope when she was supposed to be inspecting parts.

Here is an example of the expertise of their inspectors: I was discussing a call out on a blueprint with a fellow temp, someone I considered an equal. It was a symbol used in a specific type of tolerancing a feature on a print. The symbol is for symmetry: it is three parallel, horizontal lines, with the center line slightly longer than the upper and lower lines. This symbol is calling out that the identified dimensions are to be symmetrical on either side of a centerline.

Another symbol is parallelism. This is two parallel, diagonal lines. The obvious meaning is that two identified features need to be parallel to each other within the given tolerance zone.

While we were discussing the symmetry callout, one of the permanent inspectors interjected and said, "Oh, you guys. We just call that parallel!"

These are two extremely different aspects. She had no idea what she was verifying, but yet all she had to record on the inspection report was either *P* or *F*, "pass" or "fail."

One more example of their collective expertise: I overheard an engineer pose a question to one of the full-time, permanent employees. He asked, "When you see a circle on a blueprint, how do you know if it's a hole or a post?" I almost did a spit take when I heard him ask it. Later, I found out he was an intern or an apprentice or something, but still, you have to at least have a clue!

One of my fellow temps was actually reprimanded for inspecting a part too fast. The accusation was that he might miss something by trying to go too quickly. (They thought he was trying to show up the regular inspectors.) They cited the part that a full-timer was supposed to be inspecting while she was polishing her fingernails. It took her three hours to inspect that job when it only took an hour and a half for my fellow temp.

I was originally hired as a permanent temporary employee. Try to digest that! Yes, I was misled to think the position was temp to hire when they described it as temp to permanent. I found out ninety days into my employment when I asked my boss if they were ready to hire me on.

She asked, "What do you mean?"

I said, "Well, I've been here three months. It was temp to hire."

She said, "No, it was temp to permanent. You're a permanent temp."

Moving along, it was a little weird from the start. The ad was placed by the *engineering* department for an inspector. That was curious right off the top. The gist of it was that they needed a person on the inside—an inspector to help weed out the inconsistencies in the inspection department. Someone who could determine if things were being done as they were supposed to be as far as understanding what dimensions to check, how to check them and if there were procedures/directions that needed to be altered or tweaked in the instructions, etc. Someone to try to fix what was broken in the receiving department.

The reason they had to go about it this way was because of a methodology for inspection they had to adhere to called ISO. This was developed in Europe to help put all the different countries on the same page. The idea was to provide a general guideline to help control how each company in the different countries manufactured and inspected products to the same basic set of rules and held the same standards. Beyond that, using the guide, each company would spell out how they were going to do something so they could do it the exact same way every time for repeatability. The bottom line was "Say what you do, and then do what you say."

ISO stands for International Organization of Standardization.

Did you pick up on that? In most other countries, they put the subject or noun first, like *La Casa Blanca*. We Americans would say that as "the White House," not "the House White," so we couldn't even get together on the freaking name! And this is supposed to get us all on the same page!

Anyway, the way this company was set up was, if the inspector had an issue, (s)he was supposed to report it to engineering to have them resolve it. The engineering department was suspicious that there *were* issues that needed to be addressed, but no one was bringing anything to their attention, so their hands were tied! Because of the verbiage of their procedure and the requirement for repeatability, they were not allowed to initiate any conversations with the inspection department. Pretty ridiculous, huh? That was back in the late nineties, when ISO was set up like that. Since then, they changed the rules because they realized how ridiculous it was to lock you in, so they initiated a thing called continuous improvement. Now, instead of being locked into a procedure, you are required to constantly try to improve your system. Go figure.

Shortly after I started working there, the office manager realized that I was exceptional with my abilities for mechanical inspection (this was the hands-on physical inspection using multiple devices like calipers, micrometers, height gauges, optical comparators, etc.) I was regularly assigned parts that required an expertise in mechanical abilities, which was fine with me. I got to use my talents, which I excelled at and enjoyed doing.

Sometimes, I would get caught up and run out of my usual parts to inspect and would be assigned some less complicated parts. It was during one of these periods that I inspected a fairly simple part that was typically assigned to other employees. When I started the inspection, I soon realized that because of the extremely small size of the part, it needed special/specific setup requirements.

The part was the shape of a thick-walled pop can with a groove cut on the inside diameter. Now, take this, and shrink it down to the size of your typical ink pen insert. Yes, the tube that contains the ink! Closed on one end and open at the other.

You may be wondering, "How could you possibly inspect the groove up inside this?" The answer is, you can't. The part needed to be dissected in two different directions, lengthwise and crosswise (through the groove). And in order to do *that*, you first had to embed two different parts in an amber-like resin substance (like in *Jurassic Park*) while you milled them in both directions.

Now, using a toolmaker's microscope, you could measure the location and width of the groove in one view and the diameter of the groove in the other view.

So after I got involved and brought it to the engineers' attention, that is exactly what they did.

This was a fairly new part and had only been inspected by one other inspector three or four times. The way the inspection results were recorded was as "Pass" or "Fail." So for all the dimensions on the inspection report, the only thing recorded was P or F.

Guess what? Everything passed! She had results for every dimension on the print even though it was physically impossible to reach those attributes. Pretty amazing! When they asked her how she measured the part, she just said that she couldn't remember, and that was that. No follow-up on how she falsified a document. No reprimand. Her forgetting was good enough for our boss. But rest assured, like I said earlier, the parts were (probably) always in tolerance.

So let's get back to the reason why I was hired through the engineering department: they wanted a person on the inside to report to them any and all discrepancies that needed to be dealt with. Soon after I got familiarized with the system and got more comfortable, I started initializing reports on their format designed specifically for this. I would point out that a dimension called out was really a diameter in this view, not a radius in that view, or the way they were checking a feature was opposite from how they were supposed to, plus the things like the example I gave previously about how it was physically impossible to check a feature.

It got to the point where I was turning in reports about once a week. It also got to the point where my boss was getting very frustrated with me for causing her all this extra work. She was a few years from retirement, and I was under the impression that she just wanted to coast it out until then. She would tell me to ask an engineer to look at my issue before turning it in to her to make sure it was legitimate. Then she started telling me to consult one of the inspectors who had already inspected the part prior to me so that I wasn't wasting the engineer's time.

I even initiated a conversation with her where we went back into a conference room so that we could talk in private. I asked her, "Do you want me to keep turning these in? I am getting mixed signals. You seem upset with me when I give them to you."

She told me, "No, no. You keep doing what you're doing." Then she muttered, "I just can't believe we've been doing it wrong all these years."

I remember thinking as I walked away, *Yeah, I can't believe you've been doing it wrong all these years either.*

I remember my last day there. As per her instructions, I was starting my investigation by asking the previous inspector how he came up with his results to a measurement. When he couldn't recall how he did it, he suggested I talk to a different inspector who understood it better. When she came over, she couldn't remember either. ("Couldn't remember." Yeah right.) So now I had two inspectors looking over my shoulder, trying to figure out what they did the last time when they inspected it. That's when the boss came over to see what the commotion was about. I showed her; she looked it over and said, "Well, you better go get an engineer."

When the engineer got involved, he had to bring the job back to his desk to try to figure out what was going on. In other words, it was a pretty big discrepancy, and how to fix it was confounding him.

Later that day, I was brought back into the conference room, where she and her sidekick had a discussion with me. It seems that I was wasting a lot of the engineers' time, so they had to cut me loose.

I reminded her of our meeting that I initiated about mixed signals where she told me "Keep doing what you're doing" and about me wasting the engineers' time. I said, "You mean like this morning?"

"Yes," she said.

And I exclaimed, "You told me to get him!"

It didn't matter; she had made up her mind. I was furious and beside myself with rage. Imagine being extremely good at your job, doing exactly what the job description states *and* following your immediate supervisor's dictates to the letter, and still being fired exactly for those reasons! And it wasn't the first time!

Later, I realized there could have been another reason why she was dead set on getting me out of there. The chief engineer, the most senior executive in the engineering department, caught wind of my reports and came to me with a request: he asked me to start compiling evidence for him that he could bring to his board meetings. He was fully aware that there were issues in the receiving department, but he couldn't convince the other board members that some kind of action was needed, that changes needed to be made. I was already his go-to guy, and now things were looking like I might be advancing on the fast track into the executive world!

But on the morning of my dismissal, I noticed that the folder I was collecting the information in was skewed on my shelf. I was suspicious that someone had tampered with it, and in retrospect, I realized it must have been her, my boss.

CHAPTER 7

Unbelievable Thought Processes

by Upper Management

I MAGINE THE MOST senior person in the company you work for either saying that he wants "the best and the brightest" or saying "A bad employee is better than no employee."

The latter is a quote from the top executive at a company where I worked. Technically, I'm misquoting him. He liked to talk in analogies. What he said was "A bad outfielder is better than no outfielder."

The whole premise is suspect. It implies that if you fire a bad employee, you won't replace him. So that will never happen. Second, you would probably be better off without a bad employee because you won't have that person running bad parts then have to sort them, have to remake them—hopefully good this time—after you order replacement material . . .

In this position, I was working more directly with the sales/purchasing department. They didn't quite understand why I was so nitpicky, why I would go to the depth that I did when performing receiving inspections.

All the raw materials that I received required a certification of compliance, or cert. My job was to check the cert against an inspection report and make sure that everything matched up. Many times, they didn't match precisely: "A 513 T 5" on my report would only be listed as "DOM" (drawn over mandrel) on the cert. Or "CREW" (cold rolled electric weld) would be listed as "CR."

Now, I am not saying anything bad about the inspectors before me; I'm sure they were trying to do their jobs but ran into this relaxed mentality and just quit banging their heads against the wall. But not me! It's just not in my nature.

So I would ask sales to confirm, "The report says the material needs to be . . ., and it just says . . .," and sales would just tell me, "It's all the same thing. Don't worry about it."

Our last conversation turned into a shouting match. I started it when I said, "OK, I get it. You're not used to dealing with a real inspector. I'm supposed to make sure everything matches." That's when this one agent really lost it and started treating me like I was an idiot because I wasn't familiar with these materials. Then he started with "I've been doing this job for twenty-six years." That was when I just walked away. I could see where it was heading. (Usually, when somebody starts talking about how long they've been doing something, I just come back with "And you still don't know what you're doing!") Then he yelled at me, "Do you even know what these materials are?" I shouted back, "That's not the point! The paperwork needs to match!"

A Typical Day

Can you imagine telling your boss that you can't verify a call out on a print because you don't have the right equipment and having him respond with "Just do the best you can with what we have." Do the best I can? I just told him I can't! They just don't get it!

Or how about performing a relaxed inspection because "it's just a service part." Just a service part? Oh, so the customer needs replacement parts because something broke down, but those parts aren't as important as when we are running production parts!

Or when I reject a few different parts in a row, and the foreman says to me, "What? Are you having a bad day?" Or when the parts are checking good, he says, "You must have gotten laid last night."

Or when the ISO auditor leaves after their inspection, and your boss tells you, "OK, now get those parts over to the warehouse." And you say, "But that's not the procedure. They haven't been inspected yet." And he comes back with "The auditors are done! They left the building. Now get 'em moved!"

A fellow worker wanted me to include this example: The CEO was milling through the shop and noticed my friend checking his parts in a "drop fixture" as he was instructed in the job packet. The CEO told him to stop checking the parts because, "they were late" and "the truck was on its' way".

Those were all minor compared to this next one. A most recent example would be the following: In the process of bending coolant tubes for severe-weather vehicles (ice truckers, snowmobiles, etc.), a fingernail-like sliver was created in the ID of the tube. The concern I addressed was that we could not guarantee that these slivers were all being removed. In an e-mail to my boss and the CEO I wrote (paraphrasing), "It is getting harder and harder for me to pass these parts, knowing we cannot guarantee that all the chips are getting removed. They could break loose and disrupt the flow of coolant, which, in turn, could cause a breakdown, resulting in someone being stranded or, even a worst-case scenario, a loss of life from being stranded."

All they had to do was upgrade the tooling. The tooling they were using was old and worn. My concerns were not addressed. They didn't want to invest money into something if they thought they could get away with it. It was probably after they realized that the cost of dealing with the slivers was getting more expensive than fixing the defective tooling, but not before running hundreds of potentially defective parts.

In a recent memo sent out to all employees was a comment on discretionary spending. They were trying to cut costs. They listed several examples, and one of the things listed was training. I am not making this up. They perceive training as, what, an unnecessary investment?

I could list more examples of management making stupid comments or decisions, but I am not looking to fill pages with examples. More importantly, I want to open the eyes of the general public to a cancer that might consume any one of us at any time.

You or I could be the next victim caught in a bridge collapse or using a defective product because of the poor decisions made by persons trying to save a buck and line their pockets with bonuses. I used to drive on a freeway bridge to work every day when it collapsed over a river. Luckily for me, it happened a few hours after I had crossed it, but there were many others who weren't so lucky.

CHAPTER 8

What Needs to Happen to Fix This

INSPECTORS WORK FOR the same company that makes the parts. As I've stated earlier, in an at-will employment state, if you aren't a team player, then you will be replaced. So if you don't cooperate and record what the boss tells you, then you will be in the unemployment line. I've had bosses tell me, "The customer won't accept parts if they are out of tolerance, so the numbers need to be *in*." Wouldn't that also mean that the *parts* need to be *in*?

So what can be done?

Inspectors need to be more like contract employees—more like an OSHA inspector or an ISO auditor. The manufacturer hires inspectors from a third-party company. The inspectors work for the contract company, not the manufacturer. You cannot fire an inspector without cause. If the manufacturer wants a different inspector, then they have to show some form of inadequacy, incompetence, or some other actionable issue. "Not getting along" is not good enough unless, of course, the inspector has a documented bad attitude in general, acts disrespectfully to fellow employees, etc., but *not* because he keeps rejecting parts.

These inspectors will all be trained to completely understand the minimum requirements for the applications on the jobsite they are working. What I mean by that is, not every inspector needs to know everything about everything, but they do need to know everything as it pertains to the degree of difficulty on that specific jobsite. Inspecting swing-set parts requires a lesser degree of expertise than microchips or heart valves.

The good news is, we already have the basic infrastructure in place to accommodate this enormous change. There are temp agencies and placement services all over the place. Now all we need is a mind-set change. Any company or entrepreneur can use this model to have a workforce of their own, with full-time employees contracted out to full-time positions, not temps.

But it won't be easy. No longer will an inspector be allowed to give results for a call out on a print if the manufacturer does not have the proper equipment to verify it. The only way to address these issues is to state "Cannot be verified." If the tolerance is +/-0.010" (plus or minus ten-thousandths) and it measures at +0.011", then +0.011" is what gets recorded! Only absolutely exact numbers!

And as for customer prints, if there are incorrect callouts on the prints, then that needs to be addressed in the inspection report. You can't give results for what you think they mean. If you need to check the part differently from how it's called out, then that needs to be identified. And this would be a temporary fix with a time limit until the print can be revised to correct the mistakes.

And the inspector needs to understand where there is an error, especially when it reflects how the part is used in the physical world. I'll give an example of an incorrect callout for the more advanced readers:

If you have a threaded-type part that needs to seal at the shoulder when assembled, then your *datum* cannot be the shoulder; it must be the threads. The logic behind this is that when you assemble the part, you *will* screw the part together, so the threads must be your primary *datum*. (For the layperson, a *datum* is a theoretical perfect starting point. It describes how you set up the part to inspect it.) Your primary *datum* cannot be the shoulder because you aren't going to hold the shoulder parallel to the seating surface and then try to screw it together. You're going to screw the parts together, so the shoulder needs to be the secondary *datum* perpendicular to the threads, not the other way around.

When inspecting parts like this, you *must* have dedicated inspection equipment to hold the threads on the pitch diameter (not the outside or major diameter) to mirror more exactly how the part will be used. And this equipment should be ten times more accurate than the callout on the print.

I understand this is a huge change from how things are being done now. There are very few manufacturers out there that are willing to invest the money to purchase the proper equipment to inspect parts correctly. Plus all the prints out there that will have to be revised if they are drawn incorrectly.

This may seem insurmountable, but it can and desperately needs to happen. As it stands now, if I tell a customer that I can't check a part the way it's called out on the print, they don't grasp the problem. As far as they're concerned, other suppliers have made the part for them, so what's my problem? Then you run the risk of them going to another supplier.

And all these issues can be verified simply by turning to the manuals. There is no room for multiple interpretations; there are only definitions and rules that are spelled out in the geometric tolerancing books.

This is what absolutely has to happen. Inspectors *cannot* be employees of the manufacturer or there can be a conflict of interest. This is the only way to maintain a check and balance between manufacturing and inspection and to ensure that the inspectors don't get forced under duress to fudge the numbers because "they're only a little out" and "the part will work just fine."

This will force all the manufacturers to obtain all the inspection equipment necessary to check the parts or at least force them to send the parts to an outside service that can inspect the parts properly. And it will force all the companies ordering these parts to have correct blueprints without mistakes or poor callouts.

But the only way this is going to happen is if the consumer demands it. Demand that you will only purchase products that have been fabricated through this more advanced and properly controlled system. Force their hands to do the right thing. Of course, they will all say that it will drive the costs up (you know, to make it right in the first place), but what would you rather have: an air bag that explodes and sends shrapnel into your face, or the peace of mind that the next time you are on a roller coaster with your kids, you don't have to worry about any parts falling off?

The Beginning

INDEX

F

FBI (Federal Bureau of Investigation), 24, 29, 31
flash, 13
foreman, 8, 16, 25–26, 29, 41
foundry, 10, 12–13
  aluminum, 12

G

grenade, 12–13

H

hatches, 18
heat treating, 26
hoists, 18–19
hole, 4, 34

I

in-process inspector, 16
inspection, ix, xi, 1, 4–8, 14, 16–17, 21, 24–30, 33–37, 40–41, 44–45
  final, 27
  first-article, 7
  mechanical, 36
  physical, 36
  routine, 18
  spot, 14
inspection department, 7, 35–36
inspection devices, 4
inspection equipment, ix, 45
  dedicated, 44
inspection form, 7, 24
inspection office, 8, 25, 29
inspection plan, 14
inspection report, 5–6, 34, 37, 40, 44

inspection results, 37
inspector, ix, xi, 4–6, 15–16, 18–19, 28–30, 33–38, 41, 43–44
  roving, 16
  senior, 29
  source, 28
inspectors, iii, viii–ix, xi, 4–8, 15–19, 25, 27–28, 30, 32, 34–38, 40, 43–45
  fellow, ix, 6, 32
  permanent, 34
  regular, 35
ISO (International Organization of Standardization), 35–36, 41, 43

K

knowledge, 6, 16

L

liquid honing, 8–9

M

machines, 4, 7, 16
machine shop, 3–4, 11, 33
machining, ix, 11, 15–17, 26–27
machinists, ix, 5, 25
management, vii, 3, 6, 13, 25, 40, 42
  upper, vii, 3, 13, 40
manufacturers, 43–45
medical field, 33
metallurgist, 11, 20–21
middleman, 11
molds, 10–12
money, 9, 13, 42, 45

N

nonconformances, 4, 13, 21

FRANK SNOWDEN-BRUBAKER

O

operators, 4, 7, 12, 15, 17, 25
  machine, 7, 16
OSHA (Occupational Safety and Health
    Administration), 21

P

paint, 8–9, 19, 28
parallelism, x, 34
pins, 21–22
  inner, 22
  outer, 22
placement, 44
platers, 21, 28–29
plating, 20–22, 27
  electroless, 20
  electroless nickel, 20
plating tolerance, 22
president, 22, 25
pressure mic, 16
production, 27
profit margin, vii, 5
profits, vii, 5, 12–13, 25
prototype, 26, 29

Q

quality assurance, 4, 10

R

repairs, weld, 11
roller coaster, i, xi, 1–7, 9, 11, 13, 17, 19,
    21, 23, 25, 27, 29, 31, 45

S

sales, 40–41

silica, 10
silicosis, 10
slider, 12–13
slivers, 42
spray paint, 28
submarine, 18
supplier, 5–6, 45
symmetry, 34

T

team player, ix, xi, 5, 9, 30, 43
temps, 13, 34–35, 44
  fellow, 34–35
tolerance, x, 3–4, 6–7, 13, 15–17, 21–22,
    24, 27, 29–30, 34, 37, 43–44
  in, 6
  tight, 3–4
tolerance zone, x, 34
tolerancing, 34
  geometric, ix–x, 45
tools, 17–18, 33
trains, 1–2
  coaster, 1–2

U

unemployment, 12, 22, 30, 43
upper management, vii, 3, 13, 40

V

valves, 10–11
vice president, 8–9

W

weld, 11, 29, 40
welders, 27, 29
workforce, 7, 44

Printed in the United States
By Bookmasters